homespa

JENNIE HARDING

This is a Parragon Book
This edition published in 2005

Parragon
Queen Street House
4 Queen Street
Bath BA1 1HE, UK

ISBN: 1-40545-608-6

Printed in China

Produced by the Bridgewater Book Company Ltd

Photographer: Calvey Taylor-Haw

PICTURE CREDITS:

Corbis: p.4 Rob Lewine; p.5 Jutta Klee; p.16, 23 Larry Williams;
p.34 Ariel Skelley; p.42 Layne Kennedy; p.44 Mark M. Lawrence;
p.49 Joaquin Palting; p.53 Chris Hellier; p.56 Richard T. Nowitz.

This book is dedicated to Rosie and Bill with love and thanks.

CONTENTS

INTRODUCTION 4

WHAT YOU WILL NEED 6

HOME SPA ROUTINES 16

ROUTINE 1: Wake Up and Go in 30 Minutes 18–21

ROUTINE 2: Girlie Spa Day 22–33

ROUTINE 3: Solo Spa Day 34–41

ROUTINE 4: Two-hour Evening Spa 42–49

HOME SPA INGREDIENTS 50

GLOSSARY 64

INTRODUCTION

How often do you really take time out? As we try to cram more work and activities into our lives, it is important to stop sometimes, although this usually doesn't happen often enough. Going to a gym can be a way of unwinding, but exercise can often increase feelings of tiredness, especially if you don't include some relaxation time afterwards. Exercise and relaxation need to be in balance so that they can assist your body to recover from the challenges of everyday life.

In a spa – a place providing health-giving treatments, exercise and relaxation – this balance can easily be experienced. A spa is a place of retreat where you can choose from a range of activities to create a balance between effort and rest. Both of these aspects are vital to your body. Effort through exercise builds muscle and stamina, while rest and relaxation allow repair and rejuvenation.

Different spa treatments help to cleanse and revitalize body and mind. The use of water – **HYDROTHERAPY** – cleanses the skin, stimulates blood flow and assists the body to detoxify itself.

Various types of massage – **BODY THERAPY** – ease out physical tensions and assist the body's process of repair. Outdoor exercise is particularly recommended as a way of filling the lungs with rejuvenating oxygen. Finally, cleansing foods and drinks are provided – **DIETARY THERAPY** – to cleanse the system from inside.

The role of nature in the process of cleansing is vital, feeding all the senses – sight, hearing, touch, taste and smell – and bringing a sense of peace and tranquillity. For this reason, many famous spas are situated in beautiful countryside, in mountain scenery or by the sea. A spa is one of the most holistic ways of treating your whole self to a true and complete rest.

Since for many of us a trip to a spa is unaffordable, in either time or money, this book, **HOME SPA: BODY, MIND, SPIRIT**, will show you how to create a spa setting in your own home. Learn to give yourself, your partner and your friends the experience of natural spa treatments, have fun making your own spa recipes and take time out to nurture and pamper yourself the home spa way.

SAFETY – though all ingredients used in this book are natural, it is still important to follow the safety tips on page 11.

WHAT YOU WILL NEED

Your home spa will need to be organized, but this can be part of the fun and anticipation of the time you will spend pampering and caring for yourself. See it all as part of the process of creating a healthy, happy and energized new you. Home spa time will encourage you to make health care part of your everyday life, especially if you do it regularly. Listed below are some of the key elements you will need to think about.

TIME

How much time do you want to give yourself? That means time away from distractions – including the phone and the TV. Home spa time means total retreat – putting on the answerphone, switching off your mobile, and telling your family not to disturb you for a specified time. Isolating yourself in this way is the biggest challenge when using your own home, and you need to be firm about it. The routines are designed to fit into anyone's schedule – no matter how busy they are. They range from just a simple shower routine, right through to one-day programmes.

PLANNING

Think ahead – and be creative. Check your diary; later in the book there is an overview of 4 routines to give you an idea of their content; this should make it easy to choose which one is right for you. They will all fit into an evening or a day off.

Once you have decided, you will find 'menus' for your chosen programmes with suggested lists of ingredients you will need. It's best to get everything together in advance so that you don't have to dash to the supermarket in the middle of it all.

WATER

This is your inner cleanser. Water is crucial in a home spa, both for hydrotherapy and for internal cleansing. You need to drink at least 8 large glasses of water during a one-day programme, so it is very important to have plentiful supplies of mineral water on hand. If you don't like drinking water on its own, for the home spa experience buy yourself a beautiful glass to drink it from – it really does make a difference – and make sure the water is deliciously chilled. Water should be drunk plain, without slices of lemon, to give your kidneys the full detoxifying benefit.

SETTING UP YOUR SPACE

Your home is going to be used in a very different way during a home spa, so you need to get it ready. This is a space-clearing exercise to be done as part of your preparation; you will notice that the energy of your home improves even before you begin your home spa time, changing from 'normal' to 'special'. Use the ideas outlined below.

TIDYING AND CLEANING

Yes, it's a chore, but remember – this is all for your benefit. Go through your home spa space thoroughly and clear up piles of newspapers, magazines and other clutter; shake cushions, straighten throws over the sofa and give the carpet a good vacuum; dust window sills and open curtains to let in light; finally, open windows to let in fresh air. In the kitchen, tidy and clean and make sure that all the ingredients that need cold storage are in the refrigerator. Prepare the bathroom and place candles in dishes to burn while you soak in the water.

INCENSE

This purifies the air once the space is clean. There are 2 forms – stick incense needs to be secured in a suitable holder, while incense in cones can be placed on a saucer. Indian incense tends to have a sandalwood or patchouli base and smells sweet and musky; Tibetan incense often has a more earthy, forest-like aroma. Finally, Native American incense has a pine or sage aroma with a fresh, bracing effect.

FLOWERS

Fresh flowers brought into your space in lovely vases create colour, shapes and aromas: they immediately bring the beauty of nature inside. If you have a garden, you may like to select flowers you grow yourself and create your own displays; otherwise you could buy a selection and arrange them.

TEMPERATURE

This needs to be set so that the atmosphere is warm and comfortable. In autumn or winter, this will mean turning up the central heating, because you will be dressed in a robe or towels for much of the time. In spring or summer, the important thing is to ventilate your space so that it is comfortable inside, depending on the weather.

MUSIC

Have a sound system available to play relaxing and inspiring music while you enjoy your spa sessions. Choose music that is soothing, such as classical or gentle 'New Age' music with natural sounds. World music, such as Tibetan chanting or gong playing, is also very restful.

SIMPLE AROMATHERAPY

Aromatherapy is one of the tools used in the home spa setting. It uses special natural plant extracts, called essential oils, to create wonderful fragrances with beneficial effects on body and mind. Eight key essential oils have been chosen for the home spa kit, to be used in massage blends, in the bath and in facial steaming. Here the oils are introduced along with simple aromatherapy information and methods; for more detail on each individual oil, see pages 52-3.

OIL	HOME SPA USE
CARDAMOM	stimulating, warming, pain relieving
CYPRESS	skin toning, cleansing, balancing
GERANIUM	skin hydrating, soothing, nourishing
GRAPEFRUIT	cleansing, detoxifying, stimulating
JUNIPER	detoxifying, stimulating, warming
LAVENDER	soothing, skin rejuvenating, pain relieving
LEMON	cleansing, antiseptic, toning
YLANG YLANG	skin hydrating, balancing, rejuvenating

METHODS

MAKING A BLEND Take a small clean bowl. Measure 4 teaspoons carrier oil into it. Add your essential oil drops as per the recipe, stir, and the blend is ready to use.

BATHS Run the bath to a comfortable temperature, add drops of oil to a carrier, e.g. milk, as per the recipe, and swish into the water before getting in.

FACIAL STEAMING Pour near-boiling water into a heatproof glass bowl so that it is two-thirds full. Add drops of essential oil to the surface as per the recipe, lean over the bowl with your head under a towel so the steam reaches your skin, and stay there for 15 minutes.

STORING ESSENTIAL OILS

Once you open bottles of these essential oils, grapefruit and lemon will last for 6 months only, while the other 6 will last for up to 1 year. Keep them in the dark, tightly closed.

SAFETY TIPS

1 If you are pregnant, avoid juniper in any blends or bath recipes. Substitute with lavender instead. Drops of essential oil in any given recipes must be halved in the same amount of carrier oil or base, or halved for the bath.

2 If you apply a blend using either grapefruit or lemon oil in massage, avoid exposing the skin to strong sunlight or a sunbed for 12 hours after application.

3 Never swallow essential oils; use them only on the skin, in the bath or as a steam treatment. Keep out of the reach of children.

4 Always purchase essential oils in dark glass bottles with dropper inserts in the neck to dispense 1 drop at a time.

5 Never let any of the preparations get in your eyes. If this should happen, rinse immediately with warm water.

6 All the recipes are for 1 application only, unless they are made for treatments to be shared with a partner. Do not store any of the preparations, but use immediately, unless otherwise stated.

SIMPLE HERBS

Herbs are very important in the spa setting. All over the world, people of different cultures use their indigenous plants to support the health of the skin as well as the body. Mediterranean herbs are very easy to obtain and are renowned for their toning and soothing properties. They are particularly useful in the spa setting in baths and in steam treatments, as well as foot baths. Many can be obtained fresh all year round; they can also be used dried. Eight key herbs feature in the home spa kit; they are introduced here along with simple herbal methods. For more information on individual herbs, see pages 54–5.

WATER INFUSIONS (TEAS)

Place 1 teaspoon dried herbs or 2 teaspoons freshly chopped leaves/flowers in a mug. Then pour over 100 ml/3.5 fl oz near-boiling water, place a saucer over the mug and leave to infuse for 15 minutes. Hot infusions can be drunk to help digestion and inner cleansing; cold infusions can be used as skin fresheners or hair rinses. They need to be used on the day of brewing.

BATHS

If you are using dried herbs, it is best to place them in a small muslin bag, which you tie over the tap as the water runs in; use 3 teaspoons per bath. If you are using fresh herbs, simply gather a handful of fresh leaves or flowers and scatter them over the surface of the water.

FACIAL STEAMING

Pour near-boiling water into a heatproof bowl so that it is two-thirds full. If you are using a dried herb, add 1 teaspoon to the water; if you are using a fresh herb, add 2 teaspoons freshly chopped leaves or flowers to the water. Lean over the bowl into the steam with your head under a towel; stay there for 15 minutes.

BENEFITS OF USING HERBS

HERB	HOME SPA USE
MELISSA [LEMON BALM]	skin soothing, calming, restorative
MYRTLE	skin soothing, rejuvenating, refreshing
PEPPERMINT	toning, cleansing, refreshing
ROMAN CHAMOMILE	skin soothing, calming, anti-inflammatory
ROSEMARY	stimulating, warming, pain relieving
SAGE	toning, fortifying, cleansing
SWEET MARJORAM	skin soothing, restorative, calming
THYME	cleansing, refreshing, skin toning

SIMPLE HERB SAFETY

Do not exceed the stated amounts in recipes.
Herbal teas, baths and skin preparations are
safe to use during pregnancy, but do not use the
same herb for more than 3 days at a time
without consulting a qualified practitioner.

HOME SPA EQUIPMENT

Although it is not necessary to have complicated equipment for a home spa, there are some items that do increase the effectiveness of skin treatments. This is particularly important when you want to stimulate the detoxification process. It is easy to find these items in stores that specialize in health products. You do not need to have them all – a selection is enough. The following are some of the items you might want to buy.

Loofah

This is a natural sea gourd with a rough texture that softens when you wet it. It is used to stimulate the circulation in the shower; rub your shower gel or body scrub on to the skin and use the loofah in circular motions to create a skin-warming effect.

PUMICE STONE

This is a soft grey stone of volcanic origin that helps to remove calloused or very dry skin from the heels in particular. It is important to soak the feet before using it, and to massage the heels gently; always apply a rich moisturizer to follow.

FRICTION GLOVE

Often made from coarse material, this glove helps to stimulate the circulation and can be used in the bath or shower, particularly on problem areas such as the thighs or underarms. It should be used in circular motions, starting gently, and with care on sensitive skin.

CELLULITE MASSAGER

This rounded massage aid has rubber nodules on its lower surface, which help to stimulate the deeper tissue beneath the upper skin layers. It can be used with a shower gel or scrub, or with an aromatherapy massage blend, and is most often used on the thighs.

SKIN BRUSH

This soft brush is used on dry skin before a bath or shower treatment. It is particularly good for cold hands and feet. Start at the ends of the fingers and toes and brush up towards the heart in circular sweeps.

BACK BRUSH

This long-handled brush is useful to reach the back when you are in the bath; it can also be used on solo spa days to apply body scrub, improving the circulation and skin condition of areas that are hard to reach.

COOLING EYE MASK

This is a mask filled with gel, which you place in the refrigerator for at least an hour before laying it over the eye area. It reduces puffiness and helps you to relax your eyes, easing mental tension.

HOME SPA ROUTINES:
TIME TO SUIT YOUR LIFESTYLE

In the following pages you will find 4 different short routines that are designed to fit into anyone's schedule – no matter how busy they are. They range from just a simple shower routine, right through to one-day programmes, and all are packed with lush ingredients and lovely recipes to try. Here is an overview of all 4 routines to give you an idea of their content; this should make it easy to choose which one is right for you. Once you have decided, go to the relevant pages and you will find all the instructions you need to get started.

Spa treatments are a great way to keep fit and healthy. However, if you have a recognized medical condition, please consult your doctor before beginning your spa.

ROUTINE 1: Wake Up and Go in 30 Minutes
[see pages 18–21]

Turn your shower into a mini-spa session that's short enough to fit into your early morning routine but also effective at boosting your energy. Use a special shower scrub to invigorate your skin, and give yourself an in-shower acupressure scalp massage.

ROUTINE 2: Girlie Spa Day [see pages 22–33]

Enjoy a special fun day designed for a group of girls who want to spend a healthy day pampering each other with gorgeous natural foot, face and hand treatments. Try it for a pre-wedding celebration or as a special treat for someone's birthday.

ROUTINE 3: Solo Spa Day [see pages 34–41]

This is a lovely calm, relaxing day programme that enables you to unwind by yourself. This programme is a treat to the senses, with a detoxifying bath, rich massage blends and a lavish full facial treatment designed to give you a sense of deep tranquillity.

ROUTINE 4: Two-hour Evening Spa
[see pages 42–49]

This easy session, which uplifts the spirits and refreshes the mind, is a wonderful way to recover at the end of a demanding day. Try a hot oil hair treatment, a special detox shower and a wonderful neck and shoulder massage, with essential oils and herbs to create wonderful aromas all around you.

REFRESH WITH WATER

All these routines are combined with special suggestions for healthy foods, drinks and treats – cleansing you from inside out.

WAKE UP AND GO IN 30 MINUTES: A MINI SPA

C an you have a spa in 30 minutes? Yes, you can. This is a really quick and easy session that makes your shower work harder for you, deep-cleansing your skin and energizing your whole body through a scalp massage. If you don't have a shower, you can still do this routine in a bath, washing your hair in the water; just make sure that the temperature is not too hot – you want to be energized, not boiled.

The combination of skin rub and exfoliating treatment on these pages helps to stimulate the circulation immediately under the skin, which then encourages the removal of toxins through your system. Have a large glass of water after the shower to encourage elimination.

Make up the recipes in advance.

Treatments: dry skin pre-shower brush [see opposite]; shower with Grapefruit & Sea Salt Body Scrub [see opposite]; in-shower scalp massage [see page 20]; all-over body massage with Cardamom & Grapefruit Aromatherapy Skin Blend [see page 21]

Drink: Banana & Orange Smoothie, full of vitamins for energy [see page 21]

Ingredients:

dry skin brush	grapeseed carrier oil
fine sea salt	1 banana
grapefruit and cardamom	1 orange
essential oils	natural yogurt

● ● ● ● **TREATMENT ADVICE**
Use home spa treatments on the day of making. Avoid contact with the eyes. If the treatment gets into the eyes, rinse well with warm water.

PART 1

DRY SKIN BRUSHING

First, prepare your skin for the shower using a dry skin brush. The soft bristles gently stimulate and wake up your circulation. Start at the feet and make small circular motions over the toes and up the legs, towards the hips; then start at the fingertips and make circles up towards the heart. Then get in the shower and lather the skin with a good quality shower gel.

GRAPEFRUIT & SEA SALT BODY SCRUB

Place 3 tablespoons fine sea salt in a small bowl; add 6 drops grapefruit essential oil and stir in. Get in the shower but do not turn the water on yet. Take a handful of the mixture and rub it briskly all over your body, especially your thighs and stomach. Rinse off the skin well. Grapefruit is cleansing and detoxifying, and the sea salt is an excellent exfoliator, removing loose dead cells and leaving the skin glowing and ready for moisturizing.

PART 2

The second part of the in-shower mini-spa routine involves a special simple acupressure massage to the scalp. This is very useful to help wake you up physically as well as mentally. The scalp is covered with acupressure points, which stimulate energy through the meridians (the energy lines that run throughout the body). When you have dried yourself, you can then apply a nourishing but non-greasy essential oil blend, which will pamper your skin beautifully during the day. Finally, whizz up and drink a delicious, vitamin-packed Banana & Orange Smoothie.

IN-SHOWER SCALP MASSAGE

Lather your hair with a nourishing shampoo; then, while the shampoo is still on your hair, place both hands on either side of your head with your fingers above your ears. Apply pressure in tiny, firm, circular movements with all your fingertips, then move up slightly and repeat. Keep going until you have covered your whole head – your fingers will meet in the middle of your scalp. Repeat this process at least twice, and feel the energy tingle under your fingers. (This is also great for a hangover.)

CARDAMOM & GRAPEFRUIT AROMATHERAPY SKIN BLEND

Pour 4 teaspoons grapeseed carrier oil into a small bowl. Add 4 drops cardamom and 6 drops grapefruit essential oils, and stir. This is a non-greasy aromatherapy blend, thanks to the properties of grapeseed, which nourishes the skin without leaving a residue. Cardamom is a beautiful, sweet spice oil that stimulates the circulation, while grapefruit is bright and refreshing, complementing the skin scrub. Apply your blend to dry skin all over your body in soft, circular movements, especially to areas you exfoliated. It leaves the skin silky soft and should not stain your clothes. The delicate fragrance will stay with you through the day.

BANANA & ORANGE SMOOTHIE

Place 1 chopped banana, the grated rind and juice of 1 orange and 6 tablespoons natural yogurt in a blender. Whizz for a few seconds and spoon into a glass. Bananas are rich in B vitamins, as well as potassium, calcium and magnesium – vital minerals for concentration – and oranges contain vitamin C.

●●●● TREATMENT ADVICE

Use home spa treatments on the day of making. Avoid contact with the eyes. If the treatment gets into the eyes, rinse well with warm water.

GIRLIE SPA DAY: SUPER PAMPER TIME

This is a whole-day routine designed so that you and a group of friends can have a fabulous time making up natural treatment recipes and giving each other massages, as well as enjoying delicious, healthy food. This home spa session is ideal for 4 girls working in pairs, but there can be more of you if you have enough space available. Some of the treatments you give and receive in pairs while others you give to yourself.

GIRLIE SPA MENU
Make up the recipes as you go – it's part of the fun!

BREAKFAST: dishes of luscious prepared sliced fruit, for example pineapple, mango, papaya, banana, strawberries, grapes, and kiwi fruit

MORNING TREATMENTS: foot pre-treatment with Rosemary Herbal Foot Soak and Olive Oil & Lavender Foot Scrub [see pages 24–5]; foot massage with Lavender & Lemon Aromatherapy Foot Blend [see pages 26–7]; face mask treatment with Green Clay & Orange Toning Mask or Oatmeal, Yogurt & Geranium Mask [see pages 28–9]; and facial treat

routine with Infused Chamomile Toner and face massage with Geranium & Grapefruit Face Blend [see page 29]

LUNCH: a large mixed salad for everyone with plenty of raw vegetables drizzled with olive oil and lemon juice; eat it with hummus or vegetable pâté and oatcakes or rice cakes

AFTERNOON TREATMENTS: hand pre-treatment with Sugar & Lemon Exfoliating Scrub or Ylang Ylang Warm Oil Hand Soak [see page 31]; hand massage with Ylang Ylang & Lavender Hand Massage Blend [see pages 32–3]

HEALTHY SNACK SUGGESTION: a mix of dates, dried apricots, raisins and almonds

DRINK SUGGESTIONS: fresh herb teas such as peppermint or melissa; fresh fruit juices such as orange, apple or grapefruit; also drink several glasses of mineral water

INGREDIENTS:

fresh herbs –
    rosemary, melissa,
    peppermint
full cream milk
extra virgin olive oil
fine sea salt
essential oils –
    lavender, lemon,
    geranium, grapefruit
    and ylang ylang
apricot kernel
    carrier oil
green clay powder
organic oranges and
    lemons

fine oatmeal
natural yogurt
chamomile flowers
granulated sugar
fresh fruit
salad ingredients
hummus or vegetable
    pâté
rice or oatcakes
dried fruit
almonds
fruit juices
mineral water

GIRLIE SPA PART 1: FOOT SOAK AND SCRUB

It's good to start your spa day with a foot treatment because it makes you sit down and relax. Dress in a robe or a loose tracksuit so that it's easy for your partner to work with you when it's your turn. For all the foot treatments, your partner needs to sit in a comfortable chair. You will need to have ready a plastic bowl for the foot soak, some towels to dry the feet and some kitchen paper to rest them on while you apply the foot scrub and to wipe away any excess.

●●● TREATMENT ADVICE
Use home spa treatments on the day of making. Avoid contact with the eyes. If the treatment gets into the eyes, rinse well with warm water.

ROSEMARY HERBAL FOOT SOAK

Pour comfortably warm water into a plastic bowl so that it is half full. Add a handful of washed and chopped fresh rosemary leaves, and place your partner's feet in the bowl. As the leaves infuse into the liquid and bathe the feet, they gently deodorize and tone the skin. Leave the feet to soak for 15 minutes; if your partner has very dry heels, you could rub a pumice stone gently on the hard skin to smooth it. Then lift your partner's feet out on to a towel and dry them thoroughly.

As an option, you can add 6 tablespoons full cream milk to the water. This softens the skin and gives a hint of luxury. (Remember, Cleopatra was known to bathe in asses' milk.)

OLIVE OIL & LAVENDER FOOT SCRUB

In a small bowl, pour 6 tablespoons extra virgin olive oil. Add 2 teaspoons fine sea salt – as an exfoliator – and stir. Add 20 drops lavender essential oil, and stir. Rest your partner's feet on kitchen paper on top of a towel. Then carefully apply the scrub to 1 foot at a time, using small circular movements all over the foot, concentrating especially on any dry areas. The olive oil is supremely nourishing, especially to dry skin, and the lavender is also skin replenishing and

soothing. When you have done this for about 10 minutes, use the kitchen paper to wipe off any excess scrub. The feet should already feel much silkier and ready for the foot massage [see page 27].

GIRLIE SPA PART 2: FOOT TREAT

H ere is a foot massage routine that you can give your partner; it improves circulation, helps stiffness and nourishes the skin. Sit opposite your partner with a towel over your knees, resting her feet on your lap. Massage 1 foot completely first, then the other. Finally, wrap the feet in a towel and let your partner rest.

LEMON AND LAVENDER AROMATHERAPY FOOT BLEND

In a small bowl pour 4 teaspoons apricot kernel carrier oil and add 4 drops lemon and 6 drops lavender essential oils. Stir and use immediately. Apricot kernel is a light, yet rich oil that helps to heal cracked or dry skin; lavender eases aching feet and lemon gently tones.

TREATMENT ADVICE

Use home spa treatments on the day of making. Avoid contact with the eyes. If the treatment gets into the eyes, rinse well with warm water.

1 Apply at least 1 teaspoon foot blend all over the surface of the foot. Working on the upper side of the foot, use both hands to squeeze the whole area, easing out to the sides, applying firm pressure. Check with your partner that this feels comfortable. This movement eases stiffness and warms the foot.

2 Use your left hand to support the foot underneath. With your right thumb, trace steady lines of pressure from the base of the toes up towards the ankle. This may be a little tender, so be careful; these are drainage strokes, which help the lymphatic vessels in the foot. Do 3 sets of stripes, feeling carefully between the tendons.

3 Working on the lower surface of the foot, use your thumb to make slow circles of pressure over the ball, arch and heel; work from the big toe side out towards the little toe. This pressure eases out the bones in the foot, which may be cramped due to poorly fitting shoes. Firm pressure is not ticklish and should feel comfortable.

4 Just stroke the foot all over with both hands, really nurturing and nourishing all the surfaces, including the toes. This eases the foot after the first 2 sets of movements. Work the foot blend really well into any dry areas, especially the heels.

5 Using both hands, tap the foot lightly all over to stimulate the circulation, then stroke it to soothe. Repeat the whole routine on the other foot, then wrap both feet in a towel while your partner rests.

GIRLIE SPA PART 3: FACIAL CARE

Here is a lovely facial routine – mask, tone and nourish – which you give to yourself. The mask draws out impurities, the toner soothes and hydrates and the final step is an aromatherapy face massage blend. Using natural ingredients on the face is wonderfully refreshing.

A CHOICE OF MASKS
Green Clay & Orange Toning Mask
(for greasy or combination skin)

In a small bowl put 2 teaspoons green clay powder. Add the grated rind and freshly squeezed juice of an orange, and stir to a paste – add a little water if you need more liquid. The green clay is an excellent skin purifier, and the orange gently tones the pores.

Oatmeal, Yogurt & Geranium Mask
(for dry or mature skin)

In a small bowl put 2 teaspoons fine oatmeal, 3 teaspoons natural yogurt and 3 drops geranium essential oil; mix to a paste. Oatmeal is soothing and anti-inflammatory, yogurt is cooling and hydrating and geranium oil balances the skin's natural oils.

MASK APPLICATION

First, moisten the skin with warm water on a cotton wool pad. Then apply the mask all over the face, avoiding the eye area. Leave for 15 minutes, then remove with warm water and pat the skin dry.

TONE
Infused Chamomile Toner

In a small heatproof dish put 1 teaspoon dried or 2 teaspoons fresh chamomile flowers. Pour 100ml near-boiling water over them, place a saucer over the liquid and leave for 15 minutes to infuse; strain, then refrigerate. Apply to the skin with cotton wool pads to soothe the skin after the mask.

NOURISH
Geranium & Grapefruit Face Blend

In a small dish pour 4 teaspoons apricot kernel carrier oil; add 2 drops geranium and 4 drops grapefruit essential oils, and stir. Apricot kernel is a lovely light, yet rich, carrier for facial massage; geranium soothes the skin and grapefruit refreshes and tones. This gentle blend can be used on all skin types. This recipe will do 4 face treatments, so make up more blend as necessary. Apply the blend all over your face in tiny circular movements from forehead to chin. After this treatment, lie down and rest for 10 minutes – listen to some soothing music. (Melissa or peppermint herbal teas can also help you to relax.)

●●●● TREATMENT ADVICE

Use home spa treatments on the day of making. Avoid contact with the eyes. If the treatment gets into the eyes, rinse well with warm water.

GIRLIE SPA PART 4: HAND EXFOLIATION OR SOAK

It is surprising how relaxing it is to receive a hand treatment. Hands work very hard performing thousands of repetitive tasks each day; they are also exposed to many types of chemicals in soaps and detergents. The skin on the hands becomes easily dehydrated. Here you have the choice between a gentle exfoliation and a warm oil hand soak to prepare the hands for a massage. For the scrub, let your partner sit in a comfortable chair, resting her hands on a towel; for the soak, she needs to sit at a table.

SUGAR & LEMON EXFOLIATING SCRUB

This is so scrummy that you will have trouble not eating it. In a small glass bowl put 2 tablespoons granulated sugar; add the rind of 1 organic lemon and 1 tablespoon lemon juice, then 2 tablespoons apricot kernel carrier oil. Stir together. Sugar granules gently exfoliate the skin, and lemon juice and rind tone and cleanse; apricot kernel is soothing and nourishing. Apply a small amount and work gently into the hands, including all the fingers. Then wipe off any excess with a damp paper towel. This quantity should be enough to do 2 pairs of hands; make up more as needed.

YLANG YLANG WARM OIL HAND SOAK

Pour enough near-boiling water to half fill a medium-sized heatproof bowl. Then in a smaller heatproof bowl pour 4 teaspoons apricot kernel carrier and add 4 drops ylang ylang essential oil. Stand the small dish in the larger bowl of hot water to warm the oil. Then lift the small dish out of the bowl and soak each hand in the warm oil for around 5 minutes. Wipe off any excess with a damp paper towel. Ylang Ylang is a skin-conditioning essential oil that creates a lovely exotic floral aroma somewhat like jasmine. This quantity of soak will do 2 pairs of hands; you may need to re-warm it for the second person.

TREATMENT ADVICE

Use home spa treatments on the day of making. Avoid contact with the eyes. If the treatment gets into the eyes, rinse well with warm water.

GIRLIE SPA PART 5: HAND MASSAGE

This is a treat, especially after the preparation of the exfoliation or soak. Your partner needs to relax in an armchair, letting her hand rest on a towel. Sit on the same side as the hand you are massaging, so that you can be comfortable. If you have long nails, try to use the pads of your fingers rather than the tips to apply pressure.

Try a Mango & Yogurt Shake in between sessions: in a blender whizz together the flesh of 1 mango with 4 tablespoons natural yogurt and 120 ml/4 fl oz full cream milk...delicious!

YLANG YLANG & LAVENDER HAND MASSAGE BLEND

In a small bowl pour 4 teaspoons apricot kernel oil; add 3 drops ylang ylang and 7 drops lavender essential oils, and stir. In the light, rich, apricot carrier oil, ylang ylang conditions the skin and lavender eases aches and stiffness. This quantity should be enough to massage 4 pairs of hands.

TREATMENT ADVICE

Use home spa treatments on the day of making. Avoid contact with the eyes. If the treatment gets into the eyes, rinse well with warm water.

1 Gently apply half a teaspoon of the blend, stroking it all over the hand. Then use both your hands to squeeze the upper surface of your partner's hand firmly from the middle out to the sides. This eases out the bones and loosens the muscles. Check that the pressure is comfortable.

2 Still on the upper surface of your partner's hand, and supporting it underneath with your fingers, use your thumbs to make lines of steady pressure from the knuckles up towards the wrist. Work from each knuckle in turn, and repeat this sequence twice. These strokes help to encourage lymphatic drainage from the hand.

3 Supporting with 1 hand, use your other hand to squeeze and massage each of your partner's fingers and thumb in turn. Really take time over this, working the blend into the nail area as well as all over the fingers. Apricot kernel carrier is very nourishing to the cuticles and nails.

4 Turn your partner's hand over; use your thumb to make slow deep circles all the way around the surface of the palm itself. This area is full of sensitive nerve endings, so this stroke is very soothing to receive. It also eases out tension and stress from the hand.

5 Sandwich your partner's hand between both of yours and stroke both surfaces of the hand together, really warming and soothing the whole area. Ease off gently, wrap the hand in a towel and repeat the routine on the other hand.

SOLO SPA DAY: RELAX AND RETREAT

Sometimes it's simply wonderful to spend time alone. This allows you to decide what you do and when you do it, following your own internal flow. This is a one-day solo spa routine, which will help you to rediscover your own inner rhythms while you recover from the demands of everyday life. A combination of treatments, dietary suggestions, gentle exercise and relaxation will renew your body and mind. Make sure you will not be disturbed so that you receive the full benefits. The night before you begin, drink 2 or 3 glasses of mineral water an hour before bed, and try to eat lightly.

SOLO SPA MENU

Make up the recipes in advance.

FIRST THING IN THE MORNING: a mug of boiling water with a slice of lemon; this starts the cleansing process

BREAKFAST: a choice of seasonal fruit and natural yogurt sprinkled with sunflower seeds; herbal tea, such as chamomile or fennel

MORNING TREATMENTS: a detoxifying Marjoram, Rosemary & Lavender Milk Bath and a self-massage with rich aromatherapy Ylang Ylang, Lemon & Grapefruit Jojoba Body Blend [see page 37]

REST TIME: relaxation with music

LUNCH: a large raw salad with detoxifying green leaves, carrot, celery and radish, dressed with olive oil and lemon juice; choose between hard-boiled egg, hummus or vegetable pâté with your salad; follow with a choice of fresh fruit or Greek yogurt drizzled with honey

EARLY AFTERNOON: a one-hour walk in nature: spend time in your garden, go to a park or walk by the sea

LATE AFTERNOON TREATMENTS: full facial including a Chamomile & Melissa Facial Steam, an Avocado, Cypress & Lavender Nourishing Mask, an Almond, Honey & Lemon Facial Scrub, and a Melissa Herbal Toner Treatment [see pages 38–9]; followed by a special face massage routine with Geranium & Jojoba Skin Balm [see pages 40–1]

REST TIME: relaxation before dinner

DINNER: grilled chicken or salmon seasoned with lemon juice and black pepper, with 120 g /4 oz cooked plain rice and a selection of lightly steamed vegetables, such as broccoli, carrots and mangetout; follow with a dish of sliced fresh pineapple

INGREDIENTS:

fresh marjoram,
  chamomile, rosemary
  and melissa
Dead Sea mineral salts
full cream milk
lavender, ylang ylang,
  grapefruit, lemon,
  cypress and geranium
  essential oils
jojoba carrier oil
avocado
organic lemon
ground almonds

honey
seasonal fruits and salad
  ingredients
natural yogurt
sunflower seeds
chamomile or fennel
  herb tea
free-range eggs,
  hummus or vegetable
  pâté
chicken or salmon fillet
fresh vegetables
mineral water

SOLO SPA
PART 1:
GENTLE DETOX

After a gentle start to the day and a light breakfast, the first part of your solo pampering time is spent in a wonderful detoxifying bath. A combination of herbs and essential oil in the water, along with milk to soften the skin, creates a gorgeous aroma in your bathroom, and the time you spend in the water helps you to appreciate the slower pace of the day. Have some music playing while you are in the water, and even though it is morning, light a small candle – it makes the space feel very restful and special. After the bath you are going to nourish your skin with a rich aromatherapy blend.

MARJORAM, ROSEMARY & LAVENDER MILK BATH

Wash and trim a generous handful of fresh marjoram and rosemary leaves and chop them up; mix them in a saucer with 2 tablespoons Dead Sea mineral salts (these help the detoxifying process). Run the bath to a comfortable temperature, and add 6 tablespoons full cream milk to the water. Then add the salt and herb mix, and swish it into the water; finally, add 3 drops lavender essential oil before getting in. Marjoram and rosemary have a toning and relaxing effect, complemented by lavender's soothing properties. Soak and relax for at least 20 minutes. Towards the end of the bath, use a good quality soap to lather your skin.

YLANG YLANG, LEMON & GRAPEFRUIT JOJOBA BODY BLEND

Pour 4 teaspoons jojoba carrier oil into a small bowl. Add 3 drops each ylang ylang, grapefruit and lemon essential oils, and stir. This is a delicate citrus and floral blend that has an uplifting effect on the mind, while the jojoba is one of the most wonderful carriers, a liquid wax with extremely beneficial effects on all skin types – even greasy. Its golden colour gives a feeling of luxury. Dry your skin well and sit on a fluffy towel. Then, starting at your feet, apply the blend in smooth, sweeping strokes over your feet, up your legs and arms, and over your whole body. Take time over knees, elbows, heels – anywhere the skin is dry.

When you have finished, wrap up in a soft robe and shawls and rest comfortably, letting all these beneficial ingredients do their work. Drink a large glass of water. Listen to some music that encourages you to relax. Just before lunch, get dressed in loose comfortable clothes.

●●●● TREATMENT ADVICE

Use home spa treatments on the day of making. Avoid contact with the eyes. If the treatment gets into the eyes, rinse well with warm water.

SOLO SPA PART 2: FACIAL PAMPER

After lunch, you will have spent some time outside in nature; later in the afternoon, you are going to give yourself a fabulous facial. This routine – steam, mask, scrub and tone – is full of simple yet beneficial natural ingredients, which care for all skin types. It prepares the skin for the face massage on pages 40–1.

CHAMOMILE & MELISSA FACIAL STEAM

Wash and chop a handful of fresh melissa leaves and chamomile flowers. Pour near-boiling water into a medium-sized heatproof bowl until it is half full. Scatter the herbs on the surface of the water, then lean over the bowl with your face in the steam and your head under a towel. Steam opens up your pores and eliminates impurities, while melissa and chamomile are extremely soothing to the skin. Stay under the towel for about 15 minutes, then wipe your face with a damp flannel and pat it dry.

AVOCADO, CYPRESS & LAVENDER NOURISHING MASK

In a small bowl mash up the flesh of half a ripe avocado, add 1 teaspoon lemon juice, then 2 drops cypress and 3 drops lavender essential oils. Avocado is full of vitamins A, D and E, which nourish and protect the skin. Lemon juice and cypress tone the pores, and lavender soothes the skin. Apply the rich green paste all over the face, avoiding the eye area. Leave on for 15 minutes, then wash off with tepid water and pat the skin dry.

●●● TREATMENT ADVICE

Use home spa treatments on the day of making. Avoid contact with the eyes. If the treatment gets into the eyes, rinse well with warm water.

ALMOND, HONEY & LEMON FACIAL SCRUB

To make this gentle exfoliator, put 2 tablespoons ground almonds (if you are allergic to nuts, substitute fine oatmeal), 2 tablespoons good quality honey and 2 tablespoons lemon juice in a saucer. Mix together, then apply to the face in small circular movements, avoiding the eye area. Ground almonds remove dead cells and smooth the skin; honey is hydrating and lemon juice tones the pores. Leave on for 15 minutes, then wash off with warm water.

MELISSA HERBAL TONER

Prepare a melissa infusion by putting 2 tablespoons chopped fresh leaves in a small heatproof bowl. Pour over 180 ml/6 fl oz boiling water, allow to infuse for 15 minutes, strain, then refrigerate. Apply the infusion to the skin with a cotton wool pad and feel the freshening effect of the melissa.

SOLO SPA PART 3: FACIAL MASSAGE

This is a luxurious face massage, which nourishes your skin as well as working on underlying facial muscles to tone and uplift. The blend uses jojoba as a carrier – a rich, golden, liquid skin food. You should find that your skin is soft and moist after the previous preparation and ready to receive the deep nourishment of the massage. Make sure your hair is tied back off your forehead before you start the routine.

An even more luxurious version of this massage can be done with pure rose essential oil – 2 drops in 2 teaspoons jojoba carrier.

GERANIUM & JOJOBA SKIN BALM
Pour 4 teaspoons jojoba carrier oil into a small dish. Add 4 drops geranium essential oil, and stir. Geranium balances and hydrates all skin types. You can also use this blend for night-time skin massages after the end of your home spa.

TREATMENT ADVICE
Use home spa treatments on the day of making. Avoid contact with the eyes. If the treatment gets into the eyes, rinse well with warm water.

FACE MASSAGE ROUTINE

1 Take about half a teaspoon of skin balm in your hands. Starting in the middle of your forehead, apply the balm to the skin in tiny circular movements, down to your eyebrows, your temples, across your nose and cheeks and your chin. Be careful not to go into the delicate eye area. You will find the jojoba leaves the skin feeling like silk.

2 Using your index fingers only, start in the middle of your eyebrows and apply gentle pressure in a circle all around the bony eye socket area; this area contains many acupressure points that link to the lungs and the digestive system. This sequence helps elimination.

3 Continue applying gentle pressure down the sides of your nose, across your cheeks, around your mouth, down to your chin and along your jaw. This pressure also stimulates fresh blood supply to your skin. Your face should feel quite tingly.

4 Using the palms of your hands, sweep up the neck towards the chin in light, alternating, feathery movements. Use your fingertips to tap lightly all over your face, which gently stimulates the skin.

5 Gently stroke all over the face in soft circular movements to finish, feeling the softness of your skin. This kind of deep nourishment is vital for repair and renewal, whatever your skin type. The jojoba should leave no tackiness, just a smooth, even skin surface.

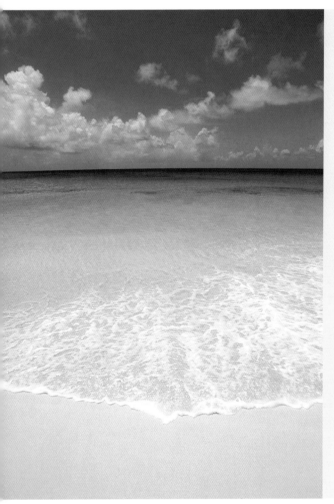

TWO-HOUR EVENING SPA: REFRESH BODY AND MIND

Here is a home spa routine that really transforms an evening into some special nurturing time. Instead of collapsing in front of the television at the end of the day, in just 2 hours you can feel transformed. Start your evening with a light but tasty dinner; this is a tonic for your taste buds and improves your mood. Then a hair wrap is a luxurious treat, especially when essential oils are also used to condition the scalp. The hair is wonderfully perfumed and soft afterwards. A toning shower with uplifting essential oils is a great way to refresh both body and mind, followed by a neck and shoulder massage to ease out daily tension, neck pain and stiffness. The evening ends with a lovely visualization exercise to help you unwind mentally; creative visualization is a wonderful technique for refreshing your thinking.

TWO-HOUR EVENING SPA MENU

Although this session is presented as a solo session, there is no reason why you could not share it with a friend or partner. You could also think about repeating it once a week as a special treat, particularly if you are having a pressurized time at work. It is amazing how a short session like this can make all the difference to your mood, your sleep and your concentration the following day. You could vary the dinner menu and alternate the shower treatment with the Marjoram, Rosemary & Lavender Milk Bath on page 37.

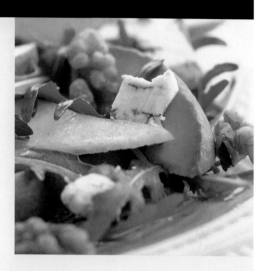

Make up the recipes in advance.

DINNER: prepare a nutritious mixed salad with avocado or smoked salmon dressed with olive oil and lemon juice; for dessert, blend the flesh of 1 papaya with 120 g/4 oz raspberries, stir in 1 teaspoon honey and 4 tablespoons natural yogurt to make a Papaya & Raspberry Whirl; drink mineral water to accompany the meal and during the session

TREATMENTS: a Cardamom Hot Oil Hair Wrap [see page 45]; a Juniper & Grapefruit Toning Shower [see page 45]; and a self-given neck and shoulder massage with Lavender & Ylang Ylang Aromatherapy Massage Blend [see pages 46–7]

VISUALIZATION EXERCISE: beach and sea [see pages 48–9]

INGREDIENTS:

jojoba and sweet	avocado or smoked
almond carrier oils	salmon
cardamom, juniper,	olive oil
grapefruit,	1 lemon
lavender and ylang	1 papaya
ylang essential oils	raspberries
unperfumed plant-	honey
based shower gel	natural yogurt
salad ingredients	mineral water

TWO-HOUR EVENING SPA PART 1: HAIR AND BODY TREATMENT

Here you will give yourself a hot oil hair treatment, sit and relax with some music, then shower it off. Hot oil treatment is extremely good for the health of the scalp: the heat opens the pores, enabling the carrier to nourish dry areas and the essential oil – in this case cardamon – to stimulate the blood flow to the hair roots, so the hair grows healthy and strong. It is also a very pleasant and relaxing treatment. Follow the instructions carefully and you will end up with wonderful silky, fragrant hair. The second part of the treatment is a Juniper & Grapefruit Toning Shower Gel; make this up before you start so that you can use it straight away.

CARDAMOM HOT OIL HAIR TREATMENT

You work the treatment into DRY hair. Pour enough boiling water into a medium-sized heatproof bowl to half fill it. Into a smaller heatproof dish pour 2 tablespoons jojoba carrier oil; add 6 drops cardamom essential oil, and stir in. Place the small dish in the medium one, resting it in the boiling water to warm the oil. Leave for 5–10 minutes, then scoop the warm fragrant oil into your hands and work it into your dry hair and scalp. When your whole head is covered, take a large piece of cling film and wrap your hair up in it like a turban. Wrap a towel around your head to finish, then sit comfortably and relax for 15 minutes, listening to some music. Your scalp will start to tingle and feel very warm. Unwrap your head carefully, take some good quality shampoo and WORK IT STRAIGHT INTO YOUR HAIR. Don't put water on before or with the shampoo, otherwise it will be very hard to get the oil out. When you have worked up a rich lather, get in the shower and rinse it all away. When you dry your hair, it will smell very fragrant.

JUNIPER & GRAPEFRUIT TONING SHOWER GEL

In a small bowl put 2 tablespoons unperfumed shower gel; add 3 drops juniper and 6 drops grapefruit essential oils, then stir together well. Juniper tones and purifies the skin, and grapefruit is cleansing and refreshing. This shower gel can be applied with a massage glove or a cellulite massager to really work it into problem areas like the hips and thighs. The bright tingling fragrance greatly uplifts the spirits. Use on the day of making. Avoid contact with the eyes. If the product gets into the eyes, rinse well with warm water.

●●● TREATMENT ADVICE

Use home spa treatments on the day of making. Avoid contact with the eyes. If the treatment gets into the eyes, rinse well with warm water.

TWO-HOUR EVENING SPA
PART 2: NECK AND SHOULDER MASSAGE

Here you wind down with a lovely simple neck and shoulder massage. To give this routine to yourself, put a towel over the back of a comfortable armchair and sit back so that you can reach your shoulders and spine more easily. You can also do this routine lying down on your bed on a towel.

Remember to drink at least 3 large glasses of water during your evening spa.

LAVENDER & YLANG YLANG AROMATHERAPY MASSAGE BLEND
Pour 4 teaspoons sweet almond carrier oil into a small bowl; add 3 drops lavender and 2 drops ylang ylang essential oils. Stir in, and the blend is ready.

TREATMENT ADVICE
Use home spa treatments on the day of making. Avoid contact with the eyes. If the treatment gets into the eyes, rinse well with warm water.

1 Lace your hands behind your neck and lean back to stretch your head and neck gently – don't force it. Then take half a teaspoon of massage blend into your hands and apply it all over your neck and shoulder area to lubricate the skin.

2 Place your fingers on either side of the bones in your neck. These cervical vertebrae carry the weight of your head; assisted by complex groups of muscles, they enable all the movements you make. Now use your fingertips to massage up and down on either side of the bones; you will feel tension easing as you work the area using tiny, precise movements. This step can help to ease headaches.

3 Try to sit so that you are well supported by the chair and your arms are relaxed. Use your fingers to knead across your shoulders; this movement can be quite deep. Your fingers will be doing the work; squeeze the muscles on either side, imagining that they are pliable like dough. Work from the neck out to the sides of the shoulders and back to the middle again, several times.

4 Now use your fingers to work as far down as you can, applying pressure in circles to work across the top of the shoulder blades and on either side of the spine. Don't force the movement: go only as far as you can; if it's too hard to do, go back and do some more shoulder kneading. Finish with some sweeping strokes over the whole area.

TWO-HOUR EVENING SPA
PART 3: VISUALIZATION EXERCISE

To end your two-hour wind-down session, here is a visualization exercise, which you might like to record so that you can listen to rather than read the instructions. This technique is excellent for calming the mind; it also focuses your attention and stimulates your creative energies. As an aid to the exercise, try vaporizing a combination of essential oils in a diffuser: 2 drops each of lemon, juniper and cardamom is very uplifting. These aromas have a positive effect on mood and help to improve concentration.

Sit comfortably in an armchair, resting your hands on your lap and your head on a cushion. Dim the lights and relax.

BEACH AND SEA VISUALIZATION EXERCISE

Imagine that you are walking on a long stretch of white sandy beach which you can see curving away towards the distant horizon. The temperature is warm and there is a gentle sea breeze. The sun is shining

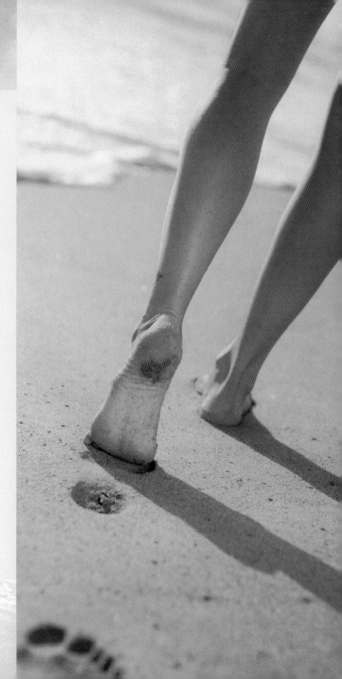

brightly and you feel very comfortable. You walk slowly, and first you become aware of the sand beneath your toes. It is warm and silky soft to the touch, and every step you take is like a caress. Tiny grains glisten on your skin as you walk along.

You turn to look at the sea. It is quite calm and a deep aquamarine blue, shining with lighter flecks of sunlight. You gaze for a few moments at the stunning blue colour, feeling it bathe your eyes. Then you walk down to the water, smelling the tang of salt, hearing the cry of seabirds and the sound of the waves. Pause for a few moments and let the scene build in your imagination; let your senses create the impressions.

Now imagine that you are going into the water, tasting the salt on your tongue and feeling the tingling, rejuvenating effect of the sea, swimming without effort, still aware of the amazing aquamarine blue colour all around you. Feel how different it is to be in it as well as seeing it. Feel yourself supported by the waves, the sun still shining brightly all around you.

Now come back to the shore and, as you leave the water, feel how refreshed and revitalized you are. Take a few slow, deep breaths, flex your toes and fingers and let your awareness come back to the room.

HOME SPA INGREDIENTS

Using totally natural ingredients is a key aspect of the home spa experience. Herbs, essential oils, salts and vegetable carriers – all of these are gently and naturally nourishing and cleansing to the system. Most of the toiletries or face products available on the market are full of artificial chemical preservatives, to which some people are becoming sensitive. Natural ingredients are simple and safe to use, though they do not keep for long periods and must be prepared and used on the same day. You will be amazed at how different your skin feels when it experiences 100 per cent natural and vital skincare – tingling and glowing with health and vitality, soft and supple.

You may already find some of the things you need in your refrigerator or kitchen cupboard; it's surprising how some of the things you eat also function very well as beauty treatments.

USING AND STORING NATURAL INGREDIENTS

Natural ingredients often have a short shelf life, which it is important to observe. Always use these items as fresh as possible in order to get the most benefit from the minerals and vitamins they contain. These benefit your digestion as well as your skin.

Items such as natural yogurt, milk or cream should always be kept refrigerated, and any treatment recipes containing them should be used fresh on the day. Milk should be full cream, as the fat content softens the skin. If you have a dairy allergy, you can use soya milk instead, although the fragrance of the recipe will be affected.

Fruits and vegetables used in recipes should ideally be organic. This is because they are unlikely to have harmful pesticide residues in their skins or flesh. Citrus fruits, for example, have beneficial essential oil in their peel, which is useful in recipes, but the value of the oil would be offset by any chemical residues. All fruit and vegetables must be washed carefully before use.

Essential oils need to be stored in a cool, dark place, with caps tightly closed. Dried herbs need to be stored in glass jars, again ideally in the dark to preserve the active properties of the herb. Fresh herbs can be picked or bought as needed and kept in water for 2 days, then discarded.

EIGHT HOME SPA ESSENTIAL OILS

Here are the 8 home spa essential oils in more detail. The information here will help you to find out more about the aromatherapy blends that feature in the home spa programmes. Also, the botanical name (in brackets) helps you to purchase the correct essential oil, as some, such as lavender, are produced from different plant species.

CARDAMOM (Elettaria cardamomum)
Oil obtained from: seeds
Safety check: no issues
Uses: stimulating and warming for poor circulation, aching muscles and sports massage; also relieves backache and stiff neck and shoulders

CYPRESS (Cupressus sempervirens)
Oil obtained from: needles and twigs
Safety check: no issues
Uses: skin toning and cleansing for oily and combination skins, detoxifying for cellulite and fluid retention; also helps poor circulation and muscular aches

GERANIUM (Pelargonium graveolens)
Oil obtained from: leaves
Safety check: no issues
Uses: balances natural skin oils for all skin types; hydrating and soothing even for sensitive or very dry skin; also helps even out combination skin

GRAPEFRUIT (Citrus paradisi)
Oil obtained from: fruit peel
Safety check: avoid strong UV light on the skin for 12 hours after massage application
Uses: helps detoxify areas of cellulite and fluid retention; useful for cleansing and toning oily or congested skin and removing excess sebum

JUNIPER (Juniperus communis)
Oil obtained from: berries
Safety check: not to be used in pregnancy
Uses: powerfully detoxifying for cellulite and fluid retention; improves the circulation, helps muscular aches; also a good cleanser for oily skin

LAVENDER (Lavandula angustifolia)
Oil obtained from: flowers and leaves
Safety check: no issues; can be used neat – 2 drops on a tissue – for acne
Uses: soothing and rejuvenating to all skin types, in cleansers and creams; also relieves muscular aches and headaches

LEMON (Citrus limonum)
Oil obtained from: fruit peel
Safety check: avoid strong UV light on the skin for 12 hours after massage application
Uses: antiseptic and cleansing properties; cleanses greasy or blemished skin; also tones up large pores and improves skin texture

YLANG YLANG (Cananga odorata)
Oil obtained from: flowers
Safety check: no issues
Uses: excellent cleanser for oily skin and hair; balances skin tone and is an excellent treatment for oily congested complexions

EIGHT KEY HOME SPA HERBS

MELISSA (Melissa officinalis)

Part used: leaves

Safety check: no issues

Uses: skin calming and restorative in baths, foot baths and facial steams; a cool infusion calms irritated skin; a hot infusion helps headaches or indigestion

The 8 key home spa herbs can be bought or grown yourself, and used either fresh or dried. Again, the botanical name (in brackets) helps you to identify the correct species to use. Growing your own herbs is very satisfying; you can then use them for health purposes as well as for flavouring food.

MYRTLE (Myrtus communis)

Part used: leaves or flowers

Safety check: no issues

Uses: refreshing and toning to the skin; the leaves are more clarifying, in the bath as well as on the face; a cool infusion of flowers soothes the skin; a hot leaf infusion is a refreshing digestive tonic

PEPPERMINT (Mentha x piperita)

Part used: leaves

Safety check: no issues

Uses: fresh and invigorating in baths, foot baths, facial steams and cleansing masks; the menthol content deodorizes the feet; an infusion helps indigestion

ROMAN CHAMOMILE (Anthemis nobilis)

Part used: flowers

Safety check: no issues

Uses: soothing and anti-inflammatory for dry and sensitive skins; excellent in facial steams and baths to cleanse the skin gently; an infusion eases headaches and stress

ROSEMARY (Rosmarinus officinalis)

Part used: leaves

Safety check: drinking rosemary infusions is not recommended in pregnancy

Uses: warms stiff muscles, especially in the bath or in foot baths; also eases pain in the joints; an infusion is a very good scalp and hair tonic

SAGE (Salvia officinalis)

Part used: leaves

Safety check: use in moderation as it has a strong effect

Uses: toning and powerfully cleansing in baths, foot baths and detoxifying skin treatments; improves the circulation and warms stiff limbs, as well as cleansing the skin

SWEET MARJORAM (Origanum marjorana)

Part used: leaves

Safety check: no issues

Uses: soothes the joints and eases muscular aches and pains, in baths or foot baths, particularly in the evening; also helps with poor sleep, soothes stress and calms indigestion

THYME (Thymus vulgaris)

Part used: leaves

Safety check: no issues

Uses: encourages sweating, so is useful in a detoxifying Epsom salts bath, where it eases aches and pains and soothes the joints; a foot bath helps aching feet

HOME SPA SALTS

Salts are a vital part of the spa experience. Sea bathing has been used as a health treatment for centuries: the salt water tones the circulation, encourages detoxification and smooths the skin. A daily dip in the sea was considered to be a major health tonic by the Ancient Greek father of modern medicine, Hippocrates. Different salts are used for different purposes in spa treatment.

DEAD SEA MINERAL SALTS

These are special salts from the Dead Sea in Israel. The water is so impregnated with minerals that if you swim there it is virtually impossible to sink. High levels of potassium, sodium and magnesium make Dead Sea salts very detoxifying; hospitals in Israel offer salt treatments for rheumatism and arthritis. The minerals are also skin soothing and rejuvenating and have been used in soaps, lotions and creams for centuries. After a Dead Sea salt bath, your skin will feel incredibly smooth and soft.

Epsom salts

This is a mineral salt with a very high magnesium content. Its effect is invigorating, encouraging the pores to open and allowing the skin to rid itself of impurities. After an Epsom salts bath, you will find that you continue to sweat, so it is important to keep yourself very warm; you may find you want to shower later. Epsom salts baths are also good for aches and pains, or after gardening.

Sea salt

Look for good quality salt from a single geographical source, such as the south of France. Sea salt comes in fine and coarse grains; for body and face scrubs, the finer grains have a less abrasive effect. Sea salt is invigorating as a treatment ingredient, stimulating local circulation and making the skin glow. Use it as a scrub in the bath or shower, or dissolve 4 tablespoons sea salt in a hot bath as a cleansing treatment, adding 2 tablespoons sage or thyme for their cleansing properties.

Seaweed

In the professional spa world, seaweeds are well-known sources of essential minerals and vitamins that assist the process of detoxification. Seaweed masks, body wraps and packs are used for deep cleansing and even weight loss. It is not easy to prepare seaweed treatments yourself at home, but you can supplement your home spa routine with quality seaweed-based body and skin products from good retail outlets.

HOME SPA CLEANSERS AND EXFOLIATORS

Cleansing and exfoliating are very important processes in a spa context. Cleansing means lifting dirt and impurities out of the skin, and exfoliating means using a more abrasive ingredient to gently rub dead cells off the surface of the skin to brighten the complexion and stimulate new cell growth. Both are needed to give the skin a really deep treatment. Natural ingredients help both cleansing and exfoliating to happen gently, without the need for harsh chemicals.

CLEANSERS

GREEN CLAY

This is a superb deep cleanser, used for making masks. It is full of minerals that detoxify the skin and also have anti-inflammatory effects. Green clay gently draws out impurities from the skin and helps to treat blemishes

HONEY

Used as a cleanser for centuries, honey is cleansing and antiseptic. Honey in face masks and cleansers helps blemished skin by preventing scarring. Use honey from a single source and try to ensure that it has not been heat-treated or blended – this destroys its active vitamin and mineral content

EXFOLIATORS

MILK

Whisk equal parts of chamomile or myrtle infusion with full cream milk to make a nourishing skin cleanser. Milk is high in protein, calcium and other minerals that make the skin soft and supple; milk baths soothe the skin. If you have a dairy allergy you can try using soya milk, but the properties are not as nourishing

NATURAL YOGURT

Natural yogurt is an excellent cooling and hydrating cleanser and can be used on all skin types; it also makes a simple and effective face mask. It is slightly acid, so it protects the upper skin layers from harmful bacteria

GRANULATED SUGAR

This has a long history of use, particularly in the Middle East. It exfoliates the skin gently and is good in body scrubs, blended with different crushed fruits

OATMEAL

Oats have traditionally been used for softening the skin and removing impurities; they also have an anti-inflammatory effect. Fine oatmeal is best for skin pastes, which gently cleanse and soothe

GROUND ALMONDS

The finely ground nuts polish and smooth the complexion, helping to nourish dry skin and eliminate blemishes. Ground almonds make good face pastes for exfoliating dry or mature skin

HOME SPA TONERS
AND SKIN SOOTHERS

After cleansing, it is important to tone the skin using a water-based product. This removes any last traces of cleanser, as well as freshening and hydrating the skin. Toners also help to close up large pores and improve the surface texture. Many commercial toners contain alcohol, which can dry the skin, so it's good to know that there are natural alternatives that work gently and efficiently. These products need to be refrigerated and used up while they are fresh (within 3 months in the case of flower waters). Aloe vera gel also features here as one of the best natural skin soothers.

FLOWER WATERS

ORANGE FLOWER WATER This is a by-product of the distillation process that produces orange blossom [neroli] essential oil. Exquisitely perfumed, it contains minute traces of the oil. It soothes and nourishes dry and mature skins, and also gently cleanses oily or combination skins. It is particularly refreshing to use after a deep cleansing face pack. Avoid contact with the eyes. If the product gets into the eyes, rinse well with warm water.

ROSE WATER True rose water is a distillation water from the production of rose essential oil. The water is the medium in which the flower petals are soaked before being heated; it contains minute traces of essential oil from the petals. Rose water has been used for centuries as a skin cooling and soothing lotion. Use it to tone and soothe dry, sensitive or mature skin. Avoid contact with the eyes. If the product gets into the eyes, rinse well with warm water.

NB: Both these flower waters need to be kept in the refrigerator and used up within 3 months.

These are toners you can make up yourself. Simply make the herbal tea using 1 teaspoon dried herb or 2 teaspoons fresh herb to 120 ml/4 fl oz boiling water, then infuse for 15 minutes, strain and pour into a clean glass bottle. Refrigerate and use over 2 days. Avoid contact with the eyes. If the product gets into the eyes, rinse well with warm water.

CHAMOMILE calms and soothes irritated or sensitive skin

LAVENDER FLOWER soothes and tones oily or combination skin

MYRTLE LEAF refreshes and tones all skin types

SUPER SKIN SOOTHER

ALOE VERA GEL Aloe vera gel is a wonderful natural product that instantly cools red, itching or sunburnt skin. Aloe vera leaves contain the juice that is made into the gel. In Jamaica, the leaves are simply picked and the liquid applied instantly to damaged skin. It is possible to buy quality aloe vera gel from health food stores; keep refrigerated and use up according to the manufacturer's guidelines

HOME SPA
CARRIER OILS

These quality fruit and vegetable oils are the best way of nourishing the skin, as well as being the medium for carrying essential oils from aromatherapy blends straight into the skin layers. When buying carrier oils, look for organic cold-pressed oils; these contain the maximum quantities of fat-soluble vitamins, which are the food your skin truly needs. During a home spa it is good to treat your body and face to these oils and let your skin absorb the benefits.

APRICOT KERNEL (Prunus armeniaca)
The seed of the apricot yields this excellent light carrier, which is very useful for face massage. It is rich in fatty acids, which nourish the upper skin layers and encourage a smooth and soft complexion. Apricot kernel is particularly good for dry, sensitive or mature skins

Grapeseed (Vitis vinifera)

The seeds from grapes yield a light green carrier oil that is one of the best for body massage, particularly if your skin is already quite supple. It is also good for massaging blemished skin because it leaves very little residue. The end result is skin with a silky soft surface

Jojoba (Simmondsia chinensis)

This wonderful golden liquid is, in fact, a wax, so it would go solid if kept in the refigerator. Keep it instead in a cool, dark place. Jojoba has the advantage of being very similar to the skin's own lubricating oils. It works very well as an oil cleanser for the face, as it dissolves dirt out of the pores. It also performs excellently as a nourishing body massage oil

Olive (Olea europea)

This is a wonderful skin lubricant with centuries of use behind it. Extra virgin olive oil is best for spa work because of the high vitamin and mineral content. It already has a distinctive aroma, and so does not work as an aromatherapy base; however, it is extremely good in body scrubs and hair wraps as an excellent nourishing ingredient. It is rich in vitamin E, which is an excellent antioxidant, therefore helping to protect skin and hair from environmental damage

Sweet almond

(Prunus amygdalus var.dulcis)

This carrier is pressed from sweet almond nuts, which, in the form of ground almonds, can also be used as a nourishing and exfoliating skin paste. Sweet almond oil contains fatty acids, which help to encourage healthy skin, hair and nails. It is very useful in body and face massage, and is especially good for dry skins

GLOSSARY

ACUPRESSURE: a system of using pressure points along specific pathways in the body to stimulate the meridians (the main energy channels in Chinese medicine)

ANTI-INFLAMMATORY: a substance that reduces inflammation

AROMATHERAPY: applying natural fragrances – essential oils – to the body in various ways

BODY THERAPY: various massage treatments designed to ease out physical tensions and assist repair

CARRIER OIL: a vegetable oil used for dissolving essential oils in aromatherapy blends

DETOXIFYING: an action that helps the elimination of toxins from the system, usually via the kidneys

DIETARY THERAPY: a spa therapy in which particular foods and drinks are provided to cleanse the system from inside

DRAINAGE: name given to massage movements in which strokes work up towards the heart, encouraging excess fluid out of the body

ESSENTIAL OIL: a liquid natural fragrance extracted from a single plant source

EXFOLIATION: a process that removes loose dead skin cells from the skin surface

HYDRATING: a substance that adds moisture when applied to the skin

HYDROTHERAPY: various spa techniques involving water for cleansing and detoxification

INFUSION: a herb soaked in boiling water (tea)

KNEADING: a massage stroke in which the muscles are squeezed like dough

PRESSURE STROKES: a massage technique for applying pressure on a small area of the body using thumbs or individual fingers

SEBUM: the skin's own natural lubricant

TONING: an action that tightens up slack skin